9-Patch Pizzazz
Fast, Fun & Finished in a Day

Judy Sisneros

C&T PUBLISHING INC.

C&T Publishing, Inc.

Text © 2006 Judy Sisneros

Artwork © 2006 C&T Publishing, Inc.

Publisher: Amy Marson

Editorial Director: Gailen Runge

Acquisitions Editor: Jan Grigsby

Editor: Cyndy Lyle Rymer

Technical Editors: Ellen Pahl and Wendy Mathson

Copyeditor/Proofreader: Wordfirm, Inc.

Cover Designer: Kristen Yenche

Book Designer: Staci Harpole, Cubic Design

Illustrator: Kirstie Pettersen

Production Assistant: Tim Manibusan

Photography: Diane Pedersen and Luke Mulks unless otherwise noted

Published by C&T Publishing, Inc., P.O. Box 1456, Lafayette, CA 94549

Library of Congress Cataloging-in-Publication Data

Sisneros, Judy

9-patch pizzazz : fast, fun & finished in a day / Judy Sisneros.

p. cm.

Includes bibliographical references and index.

ISBN 1-57120-323-0 (paper trade : alk. paper)

1. Patchwork--Patterns. 2. Quilting--Patterns. I. Title: Nine-patch pizzazz. II. Title.

TT835.S55445 2006

746.46'041--dc22

2005021137

Printed in China

20 19 18 17 16 15 14 13 12

Contents

Dedication

This book is dedicated to Ruth Breunig,
who got me hooked on quilting;
to Susie Ernst, who first hired me to teach in her shop;
and to all my wonderful students, who
encouraged me to write this book.

Introduction

Have you ever bought a beautiful large-scale fabric that you just couldn't resist but had no idea how to use? How about a panel that seemed wonderful but that now just sits in your stash? This book will help you use those treasures.

Several years ago, I bought a half-yard piece of tiger fabric. I didn't want to chop the tigers into squares or rectangles, so I knew I had to figure out a way to use them intact. My quilting motto is "Fun, Fast, and Finished," so something quick and easy was on my mind. I cut a 12½" square and a few 6½" squares and put them on my design wall. Then I chose several fabrics that had a jungle feel, all in a similar green, and went to work. The piece included three 12½" squares and several 6½" squares, along with Nine-Patch blocks of the various fabrics. The Nine-Patches blended so well, it was hard to find them! Everyone loved the quilt, so I knew I was onto something.

This style of quilt has been my most popular, and easiest, workshop. I call it the "potato chip" quilt, because you can't make just one! One student contacted me to say she has made 30 quilts, which is about how many I've made. The quilts do not all look alike, as you will see, but the premise is the same: Each quilt is a combination of solid pieces of fabric and Nine-Patch blocks (with a few Rail Fence blocks thrown in as desired). You can make these quilts with florals, scenics, juvenile prints, home decorator designs, Asian prints, or novelty fabrics—just about anything with a medium- to large-scale design. You can piece together a wall quilt in a day, including cutting, design, and sewing!

> **“Let me warn you: These quilts are addictive! Most of my students have gone on to make several.”**

Magnolia, 44" x 50" Judy Sisneros, 2002. *Full quilt on page 8.*

Anyone Can Make These Quilts

These are easy quilts—very beginner friendly, but also fun for more experienced quilters. You can piece a wallhanging or lap quilt in one day. Many students have come to me after class and admitted that this was their very first workshop, and they were hooked!

You can use any large-scale fabric. The Nine-Patch blocks do the work: they either blend in with the larger squares and rectangles or contrast so the viewer's eye moves diagonally through the quilt. The Nine-Patch is one of the most basic quilt blocks and one of the most fun to use. If you can cut strips, sew a straight seam, and measure, you can make one of these quilts! Remember, the large-scale focus fabric is the star, but the Nine-Patch blocks do the work!

You can make these quilts as wallhangings, lap quilts, or bed quilts. Try an on-point setting as well as a straight set. Examples of all are shown on the following pages. So gather some of your fabrics and enjoy!

Please read through all the chapters before beginning a project.

1

Fabric Fun

Palm Court, 50" x 56 ½", Judy Sisneros, 2004. Machine pieced and quilted.

Does the following scenario sound familiar? You bought a gorgeous large-scale fabric and have no idea what to do with it. If so, this is the book for you!

The Important First Step

Sometimes when you are in a quilt shop, a bolt of fabric will "jump off the shelf" and almost demand to go home with you. You may not have a particular quilt pattern in mind when you buy it, but you know you need it. If you are drawn to large-scale prints, get ready to use some of that stash!

Large-scale prints are fun to buy, but sometimes hard to use. You don't want to purchase a beautiful tiger print and then decapitate the tiger when you cut up the fabric. With this technique, you can use many types of large-scale fabrics. A large-scale print doesn't have to be huge—a print that features a woman 4"–6" tall is all right, but a figure 2" tall doesn't quite work.

Examples of large-scale prints

For the quilts in this book, choose a focus fabric and a minimum of three companion fabrics. The basic recipe for making these quilts includes at least the following "ingredients":

- Two 12½" x 12½" squares of focus fabric
- Two 6½" x 12½" rectangles of focus fabric
- Seven 6½" x 6½" squares from focus and companion fabric
- Nine-Patch blocks in at least two different fabric combinations
- A few Rail Fence blocks, as desired (optional)

NOTE

One of the fabrics in one of the Nine-Patch strip sets should be the focus fabric.

Focus Fabric

The star of these quilts is the focus fabric. It is used in the large squares and rectangles, in some of the 6½" squares, and in some of the Nine-Patch blocks. If you have enough fabric, you may choose to continue the focus fabric into the border (see, for example, *Fall Into Winter*, page 44).

Because it is the star, the focus fabric should be the first fabric you choose. It is best to choose a fabric that has several colors so you can include some of the colors in companion pieces. You will use the focus fabric in solid pieces and in the construction of the Nine-Patch blocks.

Suggested fabrics include:

- Large floral designs
- Landscape prints
- Large juvenile prints
- Asian designs
- Seasonal prints (Christmas/Halloween/Autumn)
- Animal prints

There is no one type of print that works best in this quilt—all of the above work great. I only use 100% cotton fabrics. However, you may use a panel or decorator print that is not cotton. If you have a panel, or a piece brought back from a glorious vacation, see pages 9–10. A panel is a printed or painted piece of fabric with a specific design on it, such as a few large fish or a Japanese or African design.

TIP

Almost every "rule" mentioned in this book can be broken. I have seen this quilt done successfully with only black and white fabrics. If that is your choice, go for it!

Companion Fabrics

In general, for wallhangings or lap quilts, you will use three fabrics in addition to the focus fabric. If you use too many fabrics, the quilt may not flow well. Companion fabrics can blend with the main piece, creating a "mooshy" look, somewhat like the look of a watercolor quilt. On the other hand, if you use a high-contrast fabric as a companion fabric, it may "dance" through the quilt. One high-contrast fabric is good if you like the effect, but use only one, unless you are making a larger quilt. A combination of blended and contrasting fabrics works well.

You may use some companion fabrics in unpieced squares and rectangles, but only if the scale and color of the print will blend well with the focus fabric. If the fabric is a tone-on-tone or reads as a solid, use it only in the Nine-Patches.

Solid Pieces

One of the things that makes these quilts so fast, fun, and easy is the use of solid squares or rectangles. With these shapes, you don't have to cut up those beautiful fabrics too much!

Focus fabric with blended companion pieces

Focus fabric with two high-contrast companion pieces

Quilts with high-contrast Nine-Patch blocks tend to be more dramatic than those with blended Nine-Patches.

Magnolia, 44" x 50" Judy Sisneros, 2002.
This is a more dramatic quilt.

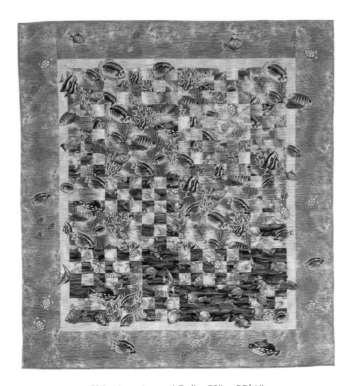

Fish Heads and Tails, 50" x 55½",
Sue Gragg, Rohnert Park, CA, 2003.
Machine pieced and appliquéd, machine quilted.

Wood Ducks, 45" x 51" Judy Sisneros, 2003.
In this quilt, the Nine-Patch blocks blend more.

Kaleidoscope I: Fractured Flight, 49" x 56",
Sandra Holt, Oakland, CA, 2004.
Machine pieced and quilted.

"Challenging" Fabrics

If you have a fabric that you have been eager to use, this may be the time to try it. Use it in a large area of your quilt if you can cut it to measure 12½", 18½", or 24½" (or any number that you can divide by 6 and then add ½"). It can be a square or rectangle. If it is an odd size, such as 14" x 21", you can add to it to create the necessary size. I brought some great hand-painted pieces back from a trip to Australia and New Zealand and added fabric strips to them to make them the correct size. See *Beyond the Reef* below.

Detail of *Beyond the Reef*, 64" x 74" Judy Sisneros, 2005.
See page 12 for full quilt.

Batik Pieces

Consider using hand-painted or batik pieces and panels in these wallhangings. Select companion fabrics to go with the special pieces.

Seascape, 54" x 49",
Carolyn Hanley, Sacramento, CA, 2004.
Machine pieced using batik panels, machine quilted.

Detail of *Jungle Fever*, 42" x 54" Judy Sisneros, 2004.
In this quilt, hand-painted parrots are combined with commercial fabrics. *See page 29 for full quilt.*

Panels

You can use a panel and trim it, or add to it, to measure 12", 18", or 24", plus a ½" seam allowance.

Detail of *Blue Bamboo*, 50" x 62" Judy Sisneros, 2004.
See page 39 for full quilt.

I hope you are getting some great ideas! Let's get started.

How Much Fabric to Buy for a Wallhanging

For a wallhanging that is 36" wide (6 blocks) by 42"–48" long (7 or 8 blocks), you need at least the following yardage:

  1 yard focus fabric
  ½ yard each of 3 companion pieces
  1 yard for border/binding

You'll use some of the focus fabric in one set of Nine-Patch blocks; these blocks will help blend the design.

The following diagram indicates a typical design, showing solid squares, rectangles, and Nine-Patches.

Sample layout for a wallhanging.
Experiment with your "ingredients." This layout uses six, not seven, small squares of the focus fabric.

2

Getting Started

Beyond the Reef, 64" x 74" Judy Sisneros, 2005.

The preparation for making this type of quilt is simple. Just cut some squares and rectangles from your focus fabric, along with strips of the focus and companion fabrics, and you are ready to sew! The cutting suggestions and guidelines that follow are for a typical wallhanging six blocks across and seven or eight blocks long. The block sizes are all based on multiples of 6". The size is about 45" × 51" or 57", including a 1¼" finished inner border and a 3" finished outer border. Projects begin on page 22.

Cutting Instructions

Always start with a new blade in your rotary cutter. It will save you time and headaches.

Before cutting the squares or rectangles, trim the selvage edge. Also, be sure to cut all pieces on the straight of grain; you don't want bias edges.

Focus Fabric

1. Cut 2 squares 12½" × 12½", being careful not to cut both pieces from the same position on the fabric. These squares will be an important part of the design. (For example, do not have the same large flower in the same place in both squares.)

2. Cut 2 rectangles 6½" × 12½". Cut these vertically or horizontally, or cut one in each direction. Cut the rectangles from 2 different areas in your fabric. These are the second most important focus pieces.

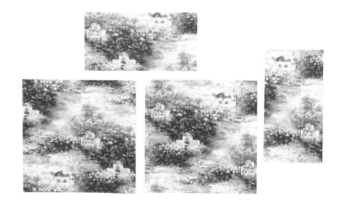

Examples of 12½" squares and 6½" x 12½" rectangles

3. Cut 4 squares 6½" × 6½", highlighting different parts of the fabric. These squares will be placed throughout the quilt.

Examples of 6½" squares cut from the same fabric

Note: If you use more than the number of the solid pieces from Steps 1–3 above, the Nine-Patch blocks won't have room to do their job. Remember, it's the Nine-Patches that move your eyes through the quilt. However, you may need a few more of these pieces, depending on the size of your design. Wait to cut until you know how many you need. Keep in mind that some 6½" pieces will be cut from companion fabrics.

TIPS

- If you have to cut up an animal in the large square, it's better to cut off the legs than the head.

- Don't make "Swiss cheese" out of your fabric! Cut some larger pieces near the edges if possible, but do not include the selvage. You need 3 strips, each 2½" x 42", for use in the Nine-Patch blocks.

- When cutting, try not to cut beyond the square. You may want to cut another piece in that area, and you won't be happy if you slice into an area you want to use next!

$4.$ Cut 3 strips 2½" x the width of the fabric. These will be used in the Nine-Patch blocks. If your strips are not at least 40" long, you may need more strips.

Companion Fabrics

$1.$ Cut 3 strips 2½" x 42" from each of 3 companion fabrics. You'll use these strips in the Nine-Patches as described in the following section.

$2.$ Cut a *total* of 3 or 4 squares 6½" × 6½" from companion fabrics that blend well with the focus fabric. You need a total of at least 7 squares (not 7 from each fabric), each 6½" × 6½", including both focus and companion fabrics. If you are planning a larger quilt, you will need more squares.

If the fabric reads as a solid, it should not be used as a solid piece; however, it can be used in the Nine-Patches.

Making the Nine-Patch Blocks

A Nine-Patch block is made up of nine squares. Each Nine-Patch has five squares of one fabric and four squares of a second fabric.

 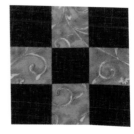

Note the position of the black squares in both of these Nine-Patch blocks.

The Nine-Patch blocks are made quickly by sewing strips together and cutting them into segments. All quilts need at least two complete "sets," each composed of two fabrics. At least one set should include the focus fabric. In some designs, you may want all of the Nine-Patch blocks to include the focus fabric, depending on your fabric selections.

"Mooshy" or "Dancing" Nine-Patch Blocks

Two different types of Nine-Patch blocks are used in these quilts—either "mooshy" or "dancing." The mooshy blocks use two fabrics that blend together, such as your focus fabric and a print companion piece. The dancing blocks include fabric that is a high contrast to its companion, such as a tone-on-tone. The dancing blocks create movement and draw your eye through the quilt. Many times both mooshy and dancing Nine-Patch blocks are used.

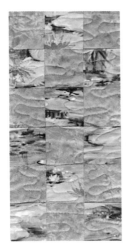
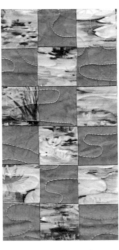

"Mooshy" Nine-Patch blocks   "Dancing" Nine-Patch blocks

Cutting Strips for Nine-Patch Blocks

1. Select 2 fabrics for the Nine-Patch set. Make a complete set before you make the next. A "set" of Nine-Patches is 10 to 11 complete Nine-Patch blocks.

2. Cut 3 strips 2½" wide from each fabric, selvage to selvage.

Sewing Strips for Nine-Patch Blocks

1. Sew 2 pairs of the 2 different 2½"-wide strips. Add a third strip of each fabric to make 2 different strip combinations.

Examples of sewn strips

TIPS

- Be mindful of how you use directional fabric when sewing the strips together. You don't want any fish to float upside down!

- Be sure to use an accurate ¼" seam. If you don't, the blocks will not measure the necessary 6½".

2. Press the seams toward the focus fabric. If your strips are 2 companion fabrics, press toward the darker fabric. You will have 1 strip set pressed inward and 1 pressed outward. By pressing this way, the seams will "nest" together when you sew the units together, making them easier to line up. Be sure not to leave any pleats or puckers when pressing.

3. Carefully align the 2 strip sets on top of each other, right sides up. Remove the selvage edge. Cut the strip sets into 2½"-wide units.

TIP

After every 5 or 6 cuts, recheck the straight edge so your pieces don't start to bow out.

4. Count the total number of pieces, but don't separate them into piles. If you have cut your strips selvage to selvage, you should have 34 pieces 2½" wide. This is enough to make 11 complete Nine-Patch blocks with 1 leftover piece.

Sewing the Nine-Patch Blocks

1. Chain stitch 11 pairs of the 2½" units, 1 of each type, flipping 1 pair over so right sides are together. **Stop sewing** when you have 11 pairs. It's easy to keep sewing those pairs together, but then you won't have any pieces left to complete the Nine-Patch blocks.

Chain-stitched pairs

2. Sew the remaining pieces to the pairs to create 2 different Nine-Patch blocks.

Note: Don't sew the final Nine-Patch block until you know which of the 2 Nine-Patch blocks you need. Since you have 1 leftover piece, either can be made as needed. If you go ahead and sew them all, sure enough, you will need the opposite!

3. Press. Which fabric did you press toward when making the strip set? Press toward the piece with 2 squares of that fabric.

Note the pressing direction for each block.

4. Repeat Steps 1–3 to make another complete set of 10 to 11 Nine-Patch blocks. You will need at least 1 more set to create the design. You'll need more sets if the quilt is larger than 6 blocks across by 7 or 8 blocks down.

Optional Rail Fence Blocks

A Rail Fence block contains three strips, each cut 2½" wide by 6½" long. These blocks can be composed of two of the fabrics used in the Nine-Patches, or they can use three different fabrics. When making Nine-Patches, you may cut a Rail Fence from the strip set before you cut the Nine-Patches. However, do not do this when using high-contrast fabrics, or else it will look like a stripe. When you have completed your quilt design and find you need "just one more" block, a Rail Fence may do the trick. A few Rail Fence blocks can also replace some Nine-Patches, but don't use too many!

Blended Rail Fence blocks

High-contrast Rail Fence blocks (not recommended)

Design Guidelines

Renoir's Garden, 44½" x 54", Judy Sisneros, 2004. Machine pieced and quilted.

Now that you have your squares and rectangles cut, plus at least two sets of Nine-Patch blocks, it's time to start designing! After the following discussion of the design process, several possible layouts are shown for various size quilts.

Design Boards

It is important to have a design surface on which to place your blocks. A good choice is a foamcore board (available at office supply or art supply stores—sometimes referred to as a "presentation board") covered with fleece, flannel, or batting. The minimum size is 32" x 40". Cardboard is not recommended—it will dull the pins and is harder to work with. A presentation board is handy to take to workshops. Place it near your machine when you are ready to sew. You can also purchase foamcore board in 4' x 8' sheets. If you have room, nail two foamcore sheets covered in batting or flannel to the wall to create a permanent design wall.

TIP

When not using your design board, store it behind the sewing room door.

Arranging the Squares and Rectangles

Following are some recommendations for placement of the design elements.

12½" × 12½" Squares

- Balance the use of larger squares. Use one large square on the left side of the quilt and one on the right. Or place one large square in the upper half of the quilt and one in the lower half.

- Do not place your large squares in the exact center of the quilt. If they are in the center, it will look more like a medallion quilt. The dominant piece should not look like a bull's-eye.

- Don't use a large square in the upper corners. A 6½" square is fine, but the large one is too heavy for the top of the quilt.

6½" × 12½" Rectangles

- Do not place the rectangles on the same level as the 12½" squares; they look better if they overlap.

- Do not place rectangles adjacent to squares.

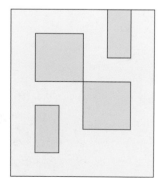

Good placement of rectangles relative to large squares

6½" × 6½" Squares

- Place solid squares evenly throughout the quilt top.

- Do not place these smaller squares adjacent to rectangles or large squares.

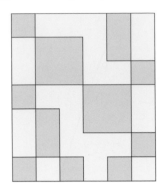

Sample placement for solid blocks

Nine-Patch Blocks

- Use high-contrast (dancing) Nine-Patch blocks to form a diagonal line through the quilt, from one side to the other. The diagonal does not have to be a straight diagonal, but it does need to start on one side and continue through to the other side or bottom of the quilt.

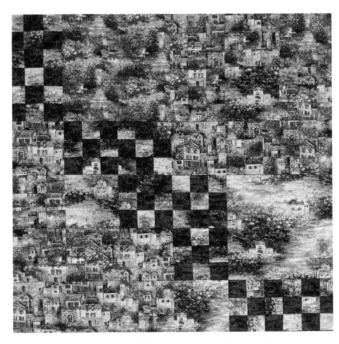

Example of high-contrast diagonal

- Place light-colored Nine-Patches toward the top.

- Position dark-colored Nine-Patches toward the bottom to anchor the quilt.

Design Suggestions

These are general guidelines for the settings of various size quilts.

Wallhangings

Try these simple block arrangements for a variety of quilt sizes.

- **6 blocks across and 7 blocks down** for a quilt approximately 36" x 42" plus borders

Pancake

29 Blocks
16 w/ those
13 greys

Design ideas for 6 blocks by 7 blocks

27 Blocks

Design ideas for 6 blocks by 8 blocks

TIP

If you are making a wallhanging and want it wider than it is long, simply rotate the design.

■ **Larger wallhanging or lap quilt:** 7 blocks across and 9 blocks down for a quilt approximately 42" x 54" plus borders

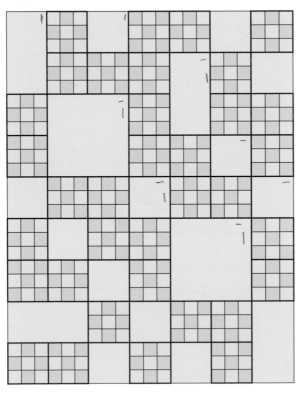

Two design ideas for 7 blocks by 9 blocks

Make a Really Big Quilt

These quilts can be made any size, as long as the measurements can be divided by 6 plus a ½" seam allowance. An easy way to make a bed-size quilt is to measure and design for the top of the mattress. Sew the top together, then add the blocks for the "drop" off the side of the bed. If you add a border to go around the top edge of the mattress, cut it 2½" wide to finish at 2". This is the size of one-third of a Nine-Patch, so the math will still work for the rest of the quilt design. Add partial Nine-Patches to create almost any size quilt.

If you are making a larger design, you may use more than one large-scale print. For a rough estimate of fabric requirements, note what is needed for the wallhangings in this book, and use that as a guide. For example, if the quilt will be twice the size, use twice the fabric amounts.

Are you thinking of the possibilities for some of those large-scale prints you have in your stash? I hope the preceding chapters have given you the tools and inspiration you need to start making those potato chips!

Lily Pond Wallhanging

Finished Size: 44½" × 50½"

Read the following instructions, and you will be ready to make your first quilt quickly and easily. Once you get the hang of it, I bet you will be tempted to make others in different sizes and themes.

Two examples of this wallhanging are shown: the first one shown above was created using both mooshy (blended) and dancing (high-contrast) Nine-Patch blocks. The second wallhanging (shown on page 23) was created with mooshy Nine-Patch blocks throughout.

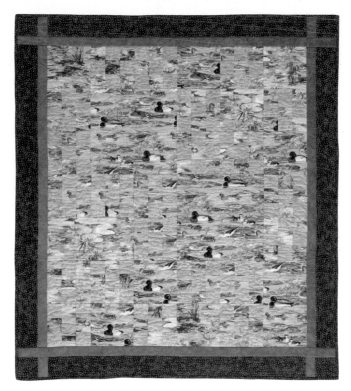

Lily Pond

The two quilts are the same size and were constructed using exactly the same size, layout, and borders. Two of the companion fabrics are also exactly the same. The focus fabrics are different, but include the same colors. After you make one of these basic quilts, try another one doing something completely different!

The fabric requirements and cutting are for the first quilt shown, with the dancing Nine-Patch blocks. Variations for the second quilt with all mooshy blocks are in parentheses.

Fabric Requirements

Focus fabric:	1 yard
Companion print:	¾ yard
Green tone-on-tone companion fabric:	⅜ yard (⅝ yard)
Pink companion fabric:	¾ yard (⅜ yard) including inner border
Border and binding:	1⅛ yards
Backing:	2¾ yards
Batting:	51" × 57"

Cutting

When cutting squares, be sure your square ruler is 6½", not 6", wide.

Focus Fabric

Cut 2 squares 12½" × 12½" from different areas of the fabric.

Cut 3 strips 2½" × the width of the fabric.*

Cut 1 vertical rectangle 6½" × 12½".

Cut 4 squares 6½" × 6½" from different areas of the fabric.

Companion Print

Cut 3 strips 2½" × the width of the fabric.*

Cut 1 horizontal rectangle 12½" × 6½" .

Cut 4 squares 6½" × 6½" from different areas of the fabric.

Green Tone-on-Tone

Cut 3 strips 2½" × the width of the fabric (or 6 strips for the mooshy version).

Pink

Cut 3 strips 2½" × the width of the fabric.* (needed for dancing Nine-Patch version only).

Cut 2 strips 1¾" × 36½".

Cut 2 strips 1¾" × 42½".*

Cut 4 rectangles 1¾" × 3½".

Cut 4 rectangles 1¾" × 4¾".

Border Fabric

Cut 2 strips 3½" × 36½".

Cut 2 strips 3½" × 42½".*

Cut 4 squares 3½" × 3½".

*Note: The cutting instructions assume your fabric is at least 42½" wide after removingselvages. If it is not, you will need to cut the following additional pieces for the Nine-Patch blocks: 2 squares 2½" x 2½" from both the focus fabric and the companion print; 1 square 2½" x 2½" from both the green tone-on-tone and pink fabrics. For the borders, cut an extra strip of the pink and the border fabrics and piece to get the length.

Making the Nine-Patch Blocks

"Dancing" Blocks

For the mooshy quilt, follow the steps below but use the green tone-on-tone fabric with the companion fabric instead of the pink. Press all seams toward the darker fabric.

1. Strip set A: Sew 1 strip of companion print between 2 strips of pink.

2. Strip set B: Sew 1 strip of pink between 2 strips of companion fabric.

3. Trim the ends of both strip sets.

TIP

When you sew strips with directional fabrics, be sure both go in the same direction. It looks okay for a flower to be upside down, but not a person or an animal.

4. Carefully layer the sets with right sides up. Cut the sets into 2½" units. You might be able to cut 17 units from each strip. If you cut only 16 units, make 1 additional strip set B unit by sewing 1 pink square between 2 companion squares.

5. Construct the Nine-Patches referring to page 15. Make 5 Nine-Patch blocks with pink (or green) in the middle and 6 of the reverse.

Make 5.   **Make 6.**

"Mooshy" Blocks

1. Strip Set A: Sew 1 strip of focus fabric between 2 strips of green.

2. Strip Set B: Sew 1 strip of green between 2 strips of focus fabric.

3. Press all seams toward the green fabric. Trim the ends of both strip sets.

4. Carefully layer the sets with right sides up. Cut the sets into 2½" units. You might be able to cut 17 units from each strip. If you cut only 16 units, make one additional Strip Set B unit by sewing 1 green tone-on-tone square between 2 focus squares.

5. Construct the Nine-Patches as before. Make 6 Nine-Patch blocks with the focus fabric in the middle and 5 of the reverse.

Make 6.   **Make 5.**

Detail of quilt with "mooshy" blocks

Look Closely!

There is something a little different about the quilt with pink dancing Nine-Patches. Did you notice it?

Three pink 2½" squares (as in the Nine-Patches) were appliquéd onto the quilt top—one in a 6½" square (upper-right corner) and two in a lower 12½" square. This helps the pink Nine-Patch blocks flow through the larger solid square. Feel free to appliqué extra squares to get the look you like.

Notice the pink diagonal "dance" and the appliquéd pink squares.

Assembly

1. Refer to the quilt assembly diagram to arrange your solid pieces and Nine-Patch blocks on the design surface.

2. Sew the blocks together (see page 44).

Adding Borders and Finishing

1. Sew a 36½" pink inner border strip to each 36½" outer border strip. Press toward the outer border. Sew a 42½" pink strip to each 42½" outer border strip. Press.

2. Sew the longer border strips to the sides of the quilt.

3. To make the corner squares, sew a 1¾" × 3½" pink strip to each 3½" square of the outer border fabric. Then sew a 1¾" × 4¾" pink strip to the adjacent side. Press the seams toward the square.

4. Sew a corner square to each 36½" border unit and sew the borders to the top and bottom of the quilt.

5. Layer the backing, batting, and quilt top. See Chapter 5, beginning on page 43, to finish your quilt.

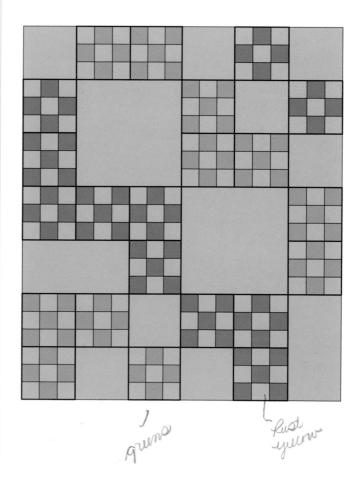

Oriental Flight

For a totally different look, try making a quilt set on point. Inspiration for this quilt came from a beautiful oriental print with flying birds. Because the birds were flying up in the fabric, they flew "across" when put on point.

Fabric Requirements

Focus fabric:	1½ yards*
Dark fabric for Nine-Patches:	½ yard
Mottled red for outer triangles:	⅝ yard
Border and binding:	1 yard
Backing:	1½ yards**
Batting:	46" x 54"

*This gives you enough to fussy cut—cut specific motifs or areas of fabric—as needed.

**Purchase 2½ yards if your backing fabric is narrower than 42" with the selvages trimmed or if you plan to piece your back to have extra yardage extend beyond the quilt top.

Cutting

Focus Fabric

Cut 2 squares 12½" x 12½" from different areas of the fabric; cut so the birds or other designs will be in the appropriate direction when placed on point.

Cut 2 strips 6½" x the width of the fabric. From these, cut 9 squares 6½" x 6½" from various areas.

Cut 6 strips 2½" x the width of the fabric.

TIP

Be sure to cut the squares on the straight of grain—the outer edges must not be bias.

Dark Fabric

Cut 6 strips 2½" x the width of the fabric.

Mottled Red Fabric

Cut 1 strip 9¾" x the width of the fabric. From this strip, cut 3 squares 9¾" x 9¾".

Cut the 9¾" squares into 4 triangles. You will need 10 of the 12 triangles cut. These are side setting triangles.

Cut 2 squares 9½" x 9½". Cut each square into 2 triangles for a total of 4 triangles. These are corner triangles.

Border Fabric

Cut 4 strips 3½" x the width of the fabric.

Making the Nine-Patch Blocks

Make all of the Nine-Patch blocks with the focus fabric and dark companion fabric. Press all the seams toward the darker fabric.

1. Strip set A: Sew 1 strip of the focus fabric between 2 strips of the dark companion fabric. Make 2 sets.

2. Strip set B: Sew 1 strip of the dark companion fabric between 2 strips of the focus fabric. Make 2 sets.

3. Press the seams toward the darker fabric. Trim the ends of each strip set.

4. Carefully layer the sets with right sides up. Cut the sets into 2½" units. You need 23 from strip set A and 19 from strip set B.

5. Construct the Nine-Patches as shown on page 15. Make 9 Nine-Patch blocks with focus fabric in the middle and 5 of the reverse.

Make 9.   **Make 5.**

Assembly

Refer to the quilt assembly diagram below to place the solid pieces and Nine-Patch blocks on the design surface. The quilt will be assembled in diagonal rows. Note the placement of the Nine-Patch blocks with dark fabric in the middle and be sure to place them in the correct position.

1. Sew the Nine-Patches and solid blocks together in diagonal rows as indicated in the quilt assembly diagram.

2. Sew the red side setting triangles to the adjoining blocks as you sew the rows.

3. After you have sewn the 6½" blocks together, sew row 2 to row 3, then to the large square on the right. Add to row 5.

4. Sew row 6 to row 7, then to the large square on the left. Add to row 4.

5. Sew row 8 to row 9.

6. Sew row 1 to the combined rows 2, 3, and 5. Continue until all the rows are sewn together, excluding the large corner triangles.

7. Attach the large corner triangles with tails extending ¼" on each end. Begin sewing at the "V" where the two fabrics meet. Press toward the triangle.

Adding Borders and Finishing

1. Measure the length of your quilt through the center and cut 2 border strips this length. You may need to cut another strip and piece the borders to get this length. Sew to the sides of the quilt and press toward the borders.

2. Measure the width of your quilt through the center, including the side borders. Trim the remaining border strips to this measurement. Add to the top and bottom of the quilt. Press toward the borders.

3. Layer the backing, batting, and quilt top. See Chapter 5, beginning on page 43 to finish your quilt.

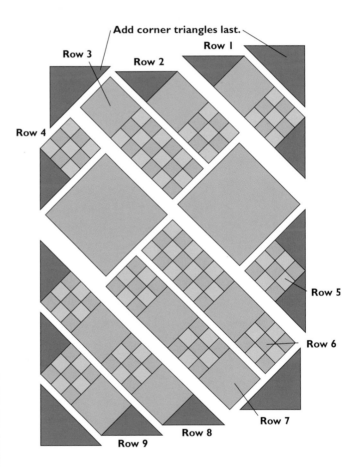

Quilt Assembly Diagram

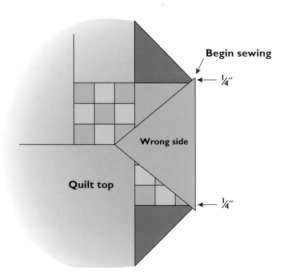

Add the corner triangles.

Jungle Fever

Many batik panels are available: flowers, birds, animals, oriental designs, and so on. This quilt incorporates two large rectangular batik panels with Nine-Patch blocks and smaller squares.

Fabric Requirements

2 large batik panels of parrots

Jungle/parrot fabric:	¾ yard
Dark brown tone-on-tone:	⅞ yard
Bright orange:	⅞ yard (includes narrow border)
Border and binding:	1 yard
Backing:	2¾ yards
Batting:	48" x 60"

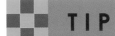

TIP

Try not to use solids. The slight variations in intensity in tone-on-tone prints add interest and depth to the quilt.

Cutting

Trim each batik panel to 12½" x 18½".

Jungle/Parrot Fabric

Cut 1 strip 12½" x the width of the fabric. From this strip, cut 2 vertical rectangles, each 6½" x 12½", and 4 squares 6½" x 6½". Cut each piece from different areas of the fabric so they are not all the same.

Cut 4 strips 2½" x the width of the fabric.

TIP

Make sure not to cut off the parrot's head! Some 2½" strips are used in the Nine-Patch blocks, so 1 or 2 strips can be cut first if necessary. Chopped heads are OK in strips, but not in squares or rectangles!

Dark Brown Tone-on-Tone Fabric

Cut 10 strips 2½" x the width of the fabric.

Bright Orange Fabric

Cut 6 strips 2½" x the width of the fabric.

Cut 5 strips 1¾" x the width of the fabric.

Border Fabric

Cut 5 strips 2¾" x the width of the fabric.

Making the Nine-Patch Blocks

Brown/Orange Blocks

1. Strip set A: Sew 1 strip of orange between 2 strips of brown. Make 2 sets.

2. Strip set B: Sew 1 strip of brown between 2 strips of orange. Make 2 sets.

3. Press all the seams toward the darker fabric. Trim the ends of all strip sets.

4. Carefully layer the sets, right sides up. Cut the sets into 2½" units. You should be able to cut 16 units from each strip set.

5. Construct the Nine-Patch blocks; make 8 Nine-Patch blocks with brown in the middle and 8 of the reverse.

Make 8.   **Make 8.**

Brown/Jungle Blocks

1. Strip set A: Sew 1 strip of brown between 2 strips of jungle fabric.

2. Strip set B: Sew 1 strip of jungle fabric between 2 strips of brown.

3. Cut the remaining 2 strips in half and sew 1 brown half strip to 1 jungle half strip.

4. Cut the strip set in half. Cut the 2 remaining half strips in half again. Add 1 of these strips to each short strip set to make 1 strip set with brown between 2 strips of jungle fabric (to match strip set A) and 1 with jungle fabric between 2 brown strips (to match strip set B). The strip sets will be approximately 10" long.

5. Press all the seams toward the darker fabric. Trim the ends of all the strip sets.

6. Layer the strip sets and cut into 2½" units. You will need 18 of each different unit.

7. Construct the Nine-Patch blocks. Make 6 blocks with brown in the middle and 6 of the reverse.

Make 6.

Make 6.

Assembly

1. Arrange the solid pieces and Nine-Patch blocks on your design surface as shown in the quilt diagram.

2. Sew the blocks together (see page 44).

Adding Borders and Finishing

1. Orange inner border: Cut 2 strips to measure 36½"; sew them to the top and bottom of the quilt. Cut 1 strip of orange in half. Trim the selvage edges of all the strips. Sew a half strip to each of the 2 whole strips. Press the seams open. Cut the strips to measure 51". Pin and sew a strip to each side of the quilt. Press toward the borders.

2. Outer border: Trim the selvage edges from the outer border strips. Cut 2 strips to measure 39". Pin and sew a strip to the top and bottom of the quilt. Press toward the border. Cut 1 outer border strip in half. Sew a half strip to each of the 2 remaining whole strips. Press the seams open. Cut the strips to measure 55½". Pin and sew a strip to each side of the quilt.

3. Layer the backing, batting, and quilt top. See Chapter 5, page 43, to finish your quilt.

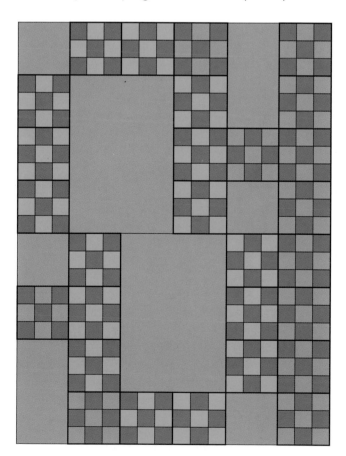

Quilt Assembly Diagram

Koi on Parade

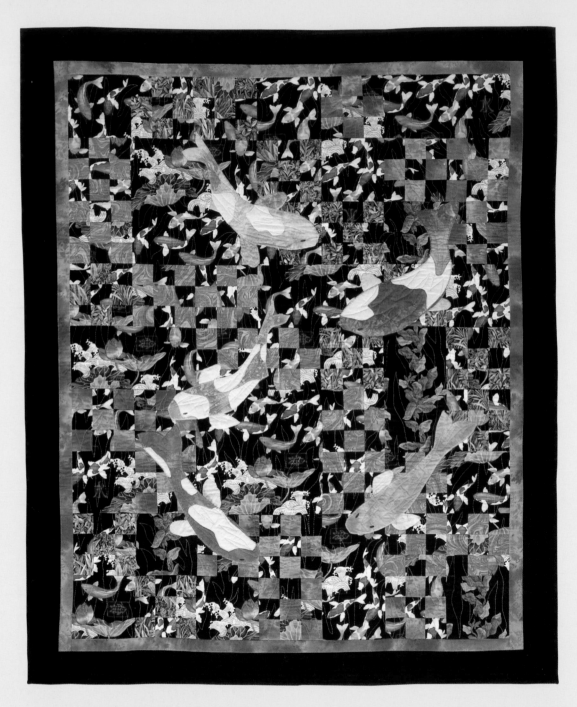

I drew the beautiful koi from this fabric onto freezer paper and enlarged them to use as an appliqué pattern. The appliquéd fish, much larger than the print fabric, add color and interest to the quilt. The appliqués were added by machine after the top was complete.

Fabric Requirements

Koi (focus) fabric:	2 yards
Orange:	3/8 yard
Green:	3/4 yard (includes narrow border)
Green "seaweed" print:	3/8 yard
Green and black print:	1/2 yard
Black:	1 1/4 yards for border and binding
Backing:	3 1/8 yards
Batting:	57" x 69"

Cutting

Koi Fabric

Cut 10 strips 2 1/2" wide x the width of the fabric.

Cut 2 squares 12 1/2" x 12 1/2".

Cut 4 rectangles 6 1/2" x 12 1/2" (3 horizontal and 1 vertical).

Cut 9 squares 6 1/2" x 6 1/2".

Orange Fabric

Cut 3 strips 2 1/2" x the width of the fabric.*

Green Fabric

Cut 3 strips 2 1/2" x the width of the fabric.*

Cut 5 strips 1 3/4" x 42" for the inner border.

Green "Seaweed" Print

Cut 5 strips 2 1/2" x the width of the fabric.

Green and Black Print

Cut 1 rectangle 6 1/2" x 12 1/2" (vertical rectangle).

Cut 2 squares 6 1/2" x 6 1/2".

Black

Cut 5 strips 3 1/2" x 42" for the outer border.

Note: The cutting instructions assume that your fabric is at least 42 1/2" wide after removing the selvages. If it is not, you will need to cut the following additional pieces for the Nine-Patch blocks: 4 squares 2 1/2" x 2 1/2" from the koi fabric; 1 square 2 1/2" x 2 1/2" from both the orange and green fabrics. For the borders, cut an extra strip of the pink and the border fabrics and piece to get the length.

Making the Nine-Patch Blocks

Koi/Orange Blocks

1. Strip set A: Sew 1 strip of orange between 2 strips of koi fabric.

2. Strip set B: Sew 1 strip of koi fabric between 2 strips of orange.

3. Press the seams toward the koi fabric. Trim the ends of both strip sets.

4. Carefully layer the sets with right sides up. Cut the sets into 2½" units. If you use full strips, you should end up with 16–17 units from each strip. If you cut only 16 units, make 1 additional strip set A unit by sewing 1 orange square between 2 koi print squares.

5. Construct the Nine-Patches; make 5 Nine-Patch blocks with orange in the middle and 6 of the reverse.

Make 5.　　　　**Make 6.**

Koi/Green Blocks

1. Strip set A: Sew 1 strip of green between 2 strips of koi fabric.

2. Strip set B: Sew 1 strip of koi fabric between 2 strips of green.

3. Press the seams of all the strip sets toward the darker fabric; trim the ends of the strip sets.

4. Layer the strip sets and cut them into 2½" units. Cut 17 from each strip set. If you cut only 16 units, make 1 additional strip set A unit by sewing 1 green square between 2 koi print squares.

5. Construct the Nine-Patches; make 5 Nine-Patch blocks with green in the middle and 6 of the reverse.

Make 5.　　　　**Make 6.**

Koi/Green "Seaweed" Blocks

1. Strip set A: Sew 1 strip of koi fabric between 2 strips of green "seaweed." Make 2 strip sets.

2. Strip set B: Sew 1 strip of green "seaweed" between 2 strips of koi fabric.

3. Press all the seams toward the darker fabric. Trim the ends, layer the strip sets, and cut into 2½" units. Cut 20 units from the A strip sets and 16 from strip set B.

4. Construct the Nine-Patches. Make 8 Nine-Patch blocks with green "seaweed" in the middle and 4 of the reverse.

Make 8.　　　　**Make 4.**

Assembly

1. Refer to the quilt assembly diagram to lay out the solid pieces and Nine-Patch blocks.

2. Sew the blocks together (see page 44). Your quilt should measure 42½" x 54½" without borders.

Adding Borders and Finishing

1. Green inner border: Trim the selvage edges of the strips. Piece if necessary and trim 2 green strips to measure 42½". Add them to the top and bottom of the quilt. Press toward the borders.

2. Piece the remaining green strips to make one long strip. Cut 2 strips each 57" long. Piece the black strips and cut 2 strips 57" long and 2 strips 51" long.

3. Pin and sew a 57" green strip to each 57" black strip. Press toward the black. Attach these pieced strips to the sides of the quilt. Press toward the borders.

4. Pin and sew a 51" black strip to the top and bottom of the quilt top. Press toward the borders.

Quilt Assembly Diagram

5. Layer the backing, batting, and quilt top. See Chapter 5, beginning on page 43, to finish your quilt.

Appliquéd Fish

You can easily add appliquéd fish to this quilt. Draw fish on freezer paper, then use them as a pattern. You can also enlarge and photocopy the fish on the fabric. If you use two or three different fish, use the pattern on the reverse side for some of the fish to make them go in different directions.

Attach the appliqués to the quilt top with a machine blanket stitch or use your preferred method. For machine appliqué, use a stabilizer under the quilt top when stitching. I stitched the body of the fish first, then added the spots.

Try not to put a fish in the center of the quilt. Use a black permanent marker to make the fish eyes. Have fun with it...your fish don't have to be perfect!

Flower Power

I t was hard for me to cut into this gorgeous floral fabric, but it was worth it! The addition of the sashing strips, paired with different sizes of rectangles and squares, lends this quilt an entirely different look and feel.

Fabric Requirements

Floral focus fabric: 1¼ yards (includes binding)

Black: 1⅛ yards

Green: 1⅛ yards

Backing: 2½ yards*

Batting: 46" x 62"

*If your fabric is wide enough, 1¾ yards may be enough.

TIP

Use tone-on-tone rather than solid black/green to add interest and texture.

Cutting

Floral Fabric

Cut 4 strips 6½" vertically (along the lengthwise grain).

From the strips, cut 7 rectangles 6½" x 12½", 1 rectangle 6½" x 8½", and 7 squares 6½" x 6½".

Black Fabric

Cut 7 strips 2½" x the width of the fabric.

Cut 10 strips 1½" x the width of the fabric.

Green Fabric

Cut 8 strips 2½" x the width of the fabric.

Cut 10 strips 1½" x the width of the fabric.

TIP

Chain piece as you sew the sashing strips. While the second unit is under the needle, clip the thread to remove the first unit, press toward the sashing, and replace it on your design surface.

Making the Sashing

1. Sew 1½"-wide black strips to 1½"-wide green strips lengthwise. Make 10 pairs.

2. Press 6 strip sets toward the black fabric and 4 strips toward the green fabric. Trim the ends of each strip set.

3. Sew together 2 strip sets pressed in opposite directions along the short ends. Trim to 56½" to make a long sashing piece. Repeat to make 4.

4. From the remaining sashing strip sets, cut 1 strip 14½" long and 17 pieces 6½" long.

Making the Nine-Patch Blocks

1. Strip set A: Sew 1 strip of black between 2 strips of green. Make 3 sets.

2. Strip set B: Sew 1 strip of green between 2 strips of black. Make 2 sets.

3. Press all seams toward the black. Trim the ends of each strip set.

4. Carefully layer 2 sets together with right sides up. Cut the sets into 2½" units. Repeat with all of the strip sets made in Steps 1 and 2. You will need 33 units from the A strip sets and 30 units from the B strip sets.

5. Construct the Nine-Patches; make 7 with black in the center and 10 of the reverse. You will need 17 complete Nine-Patch blocks. Set aside the leftover pieces.

Make 7.   **Make 10.**

Assembly

1. Refer to the quilt assembly diagram and lay out the solid pieces in vertical rows. The 6½" x 8½" rectangle goes at the top of row 4.

2. Sew a 6½" strip to the bottom of the large rectangle in row 1; sew the 14½" piece to the left side of the same rectangle.

3. Sew the 6½" sashing pieces to the squares and rectangles as shown in the diagram. Place either the black or the green next to the square or rectangle, using the color that contrasts best with that piece.

4. Place the Nine-Patches on the design surface with the solid squares and rectangles as shown.

5. Place the long sashing strips between the rows.

6. Sew together partial Nine-Patches as needed for the bottom of rows 2 and 4 and the top of row 3. Place them on the design surface.

7. Sew another unit to each of the 7 Nine-Patches in row 1 (this makes them 12-patches) and return them to the design wall.

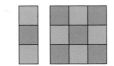

Add to the Nine-Patches.

8. Sew the pieces together in each vertical row.

9. Carefully pin the long sashing piece to the left side of each vertical row. Stitch. Press toward the sashing.

10. Pin carefully and stitch the rows together. Press toward the sashing.

NOTE

This quilt does not have a border.

11. Layer the backing, batting, and quilt top. See Chapter 5, beginning on page 43, to finish your quilt.

Quilt Assembly Diagram

Blue Bamboo

There are many beautiful, large fabric panels available. This panel was originally about 28" x 36". Note that the flow of color in the Nine-Patches goes from right to left. Japanese writing flows from right to left, so it seemed appropriate. Red Nine-Patches make the strong diagonal; the Nine-Patches with tan fabric lighten the quilt as they flow from the top.

Fabric Requirements

Large panel:	20" x 26" or larger
Dark blue indigo:	⅝ yard
Light tan:	¾ yard for Nine-Patches and binding
Red (tone-on-tone or print, not solid):	¾ yard
Multicolored print:	1⅜ yard
Blue/gray print:	1 yard
Backing:	3 yards
Batting:	57" x 69"

Cutting

Large Panel

Trim the large panel to 18½" x 24½". If there is leftover fabric, cut 2 squares 6½" x 6½".

Dark Blue Indigo Fabric

Cut 6 strips 2½" x the width of the fabric.

Light Tan Fabric

Cut 3 strips 2½" x the width of the fabric.*

Red Fabric

Cut 3 strips 2½" x the width of the fabric.

Cut 5 strips 1½" x the width of the fabric for inner border.

Multicolored Print

Cut 2 strips 6½" x the width of the fabric. From these strips, cut 1 rectangle 6½" x 12½" and 10 squares 6½" x 6½". If you did not have leftovers from the large panel, cut 2 additional 6½" x 6½" squares from the multicolored print for a total of 12.

Cut 9 strips 2½" x the width of the fabric.*

Blue/Gray Print

Cut 3 strips 2½" x the width of the fabric.

Cut 5 strips 3½" x the width of the fabric for outer border.

*Note: The cutting instructions assume that your fabric is at least 41½" wide after removing the selvages. If it is not, you will need to cut the following additional pieces for the Nine-Patch blocks: 1 square 2½" x 2½" from the red fabric; 2 squares 2½" x 2½" from the multicolored print. For the borders, cut an extra 1¾" strip of the red fabric and one additional 3½" strip of the blue/gray fabric and piece to get the length.

Making the Nine-Patch and Rail Fence Blocks

Red Fabric With Multicolored Print

1. Strip set A: Sew 1 strip of red between 2 strips of multicolored print.

2. Strip set B: Sew 1 strip of multicolored print between 2 strips of red.

3. Press all seams toward the red. Trim the ends of both strip sets.

4. Make 2 Rail Fence blocks: Cut 1 square 6½" x 6½" from both strip sets. Set aside.

5. Carefully layer the sets with right sides up. Cut into 2½" units. You need 14 units from strip set A and 13 from strip set B. If needed, make 1 additional strip set A unit by sewing a red 2½" square between 2 multicolored 2½" squares.

6. Construct the Nine-Patches, referring to page 15. Make 5 Nine-Patch blocks with the multicolored fabric in the middle and 4 of the reverse.

Make 5.

Make 4.

Tan Fabric With Multicolored Print

1. Strip set A: Sew 1 strip of tan between 2 strips of multicolored print.

2. Strip set B: Sew 1 strip of multicolored print between 2 strips of tan.

3. Press all seams toward the tan. Trim the ends of both strip sets.

4. Carefully layer the sets with right sides up. Cut into 2½" units. You need 16 from strip set A and 14 from strip set B.

5. Construct the Nine-Patches. Make 4 Nine-Patch blocks with tan in the middle and 6 of the reverse.

Make 4.

Make 6.

Dark Blue Indigo With Multicolored Print

1. Strip set A: Sew 1 strip of dark blue indigo between 2 strips of multicolored print.

2. Strip set B: Sew 1 strip of multicolored print between 2 strips of dark blue indigo.

3. Press all seams toward the dark blue indigo. Trim the ends of the strip sets.

4. Make 3 Rail Fence blocks: Cut 1 square 6½" x 6½" from the strip set with indigo in the middle. Cut 2 squares 6½" x 6½" from the strip set with the multicolored print in the middle.

5. Carefully layer the remaining strip sets with right sides up. Cut into 2½" units. You will need 4 from strip set A and 5 from strip set B.

6. Construct the Nine-Patches. Make 2 Nine-Patch blocks with indigo in the middle and 1 of the reverse.

Make 2.

Make 1.

Dark Blue Indigo With Blue/Gray Print

1. Strip set A: Sew 1 strip of dark blue indigo between 2 strips of blue/gray print.

2. Strip set B: Sew 1 strip of blue/gray print between 2 strips of dark blue indigo.

3. Press all seams toward the blue/gray print. Trim the ends.

4. Carefully layer the strip sets with right sides up. Cut into 2½" units. You will need 16 from strip set A and 14 from strip set B.

5. Construct the Nine-Patches. Make 4 Nine-Patch blocks with indigo in the middle and 6 of the reverse.

Make 4.

Make 6.

Assembly

1. Refer to the quilt assembly diagram to lay out the panel, rectangle, solid squares, and Nine-Patch blocks on your design surface.

2. Sew the blocks together (see page 44). Your quilt should measure 42½" x 54½" without borders.

Adding Borders and Finishing

1. Trim the selvage edge of all the strips.

2. Trim 2 red strips to measure 42½". Trim 2 strips of blue/gray to measure 42½". You may need to cut an additional strip of each and piece the border strips if your fabric isn't this wide after removing the selvages. Sew the red strips to the blue/gray strips.

3. Pin and sew the joined strips to the top and bottom of the quilt so the red fabric forms the inner border. Press toward the border.

4. Cut 1 strip of red and 1 strip of blue/gray print in half. Sew a half strip to each of the remaining 2 whole strips of both red and blue/gray. Press the seam open.

5. Trim 2 red strips to 63". Trim 2 blue-gray strips to 63". Sew the red strips to the blue/gray strips. Pin and sew the strips to each side of the quilt so the red fabric forms the inner border. Press toward the border.

6. Layer the backing, batting, and quilt top. See Chapter 5, beginning on page 43, to finish your quilt.

Quilt Assembly Diagram

Finishing

Fall Into Winter, 55" x 37", Judy Sisneros, 2003.
Machine pieced and quilted.

Sew the Blocks Together

Now that your design is complete, how do you sew it together? Some quilters take two blocks, sew them together, and return them to the design surface, one pair at a time. This works fine, but it is very time-consuming. I'll show you my way, then you can decide whether you want to use it. This method is definitely quicker once you get used to it.

Look at the composition of the quilt as if it were a jigsaw puzzle. You will put it together in units, depending on the design. We'll use the sewing diagram above as an example. Refer to the numbers for the horizontal rows and the letters for the vertical rows.

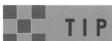

TIP

Use a neutral thread, such as gray, to blend with your fabrics.

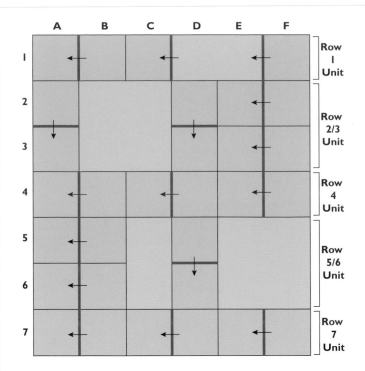

Sewing Diagram

1. Begin at the bottom left side of the quilt. Take blocks 7A and 7B and place them right sides together with block 7B on top. The side that you will stitch should be on the right, ready to place in the machine.

2. Take the next 2 blocks, 6A and 6B, placing 6B on top as you did with 7B. Place these 2 blocks on top of the first 2 blocks. Continue with rows 5 and 4, stacking them in a pile.

3. When you get to row 3, take blocks 3A and 2A, and place them right sides together with 2A on top of 3A. Turn the blocks so that the stitching line is on the right.

4. When you have added the blocks from row 1 (1A and 1B), chain stitch the blocks together in pairs, sewing the seams marked in red on the diagram in rows A and B. Cut apart, press, and place the blocks back on the design surface.

5. Stack rows C and D in the same manner, sewing the seams marked in red. Then do rows E and F.

*Note: As you stitch the blocks together, you will see that row 1 is a unit, rows 2 and 3 together are a unit, row 4 is a unit, rows 5 and 6 together are a unit, and row 7 is a unit.

6. Continue stitching until each unit is complete. Sew the units together to complete the quilt top.

TIP

As you sew the rows, press in opposite directions (such as row 1 to the left, row 2 to the right, and so on).

Square Up the Quilt Top

If you have sewn accurate seams and cut accurate blocks, you will not need to adjust the quilt. Measure across the top, middle, and bottom of the quilt. These measurements should be equal. Then measure from the top to the bottom on the left, then down the middle, and then on the right. These measurements should also be equal. If not, adjust as necessary. If you must trim off excess, divide the amount and cut half from each side. For example, if you have an extra $\frac{1}{2}$", trim $\frac{1}{4}$" from each side.

Remember: If you trim the quilt top to a smaller size, you will need to trim the border as well.

TIP

Be sure to press the quilt well. If you have some puckers where blocks are sewn together, press again before you do any cutting.

Borders

Every fabric in your quilt has a job to do—the border's job is to contain the quilt and frame it, but not distract from it. A narrow inner border cut $1\frac{3}{4}$" is a good choice. You will usually want to use a fabric that pulls out one of the strong colors in the quilt, such as red. Look through the projects and other quilts to get the idea.

If you have more of the print fabrics left when your top is complete, you may want to include them in the border. The narrow border stops the action, and the outer border continues the quilt design.

Example of quilt design carried into the border

TIPS

- Before cutting strips, be sure to straighten the fabric and trim so you have a straight edge.

- Always be sure to use an accurate $\frac{1}{4}$" seam.

In addition to the narrow inner border, I usually add a $3\frac{1}{2}$" outer border. This border often picks up the darkest color in the quilt and acts like a frame.

Often my inner borders extend through the outer borders. This method works well for several reasons.

◼ It looks nice.

◼ The corners don't have to be mitered.

◼ You can often avoid piecing the border.

As you may have noticed from my quilts, I like to use a border treatment that looks like this in the corners.

If your quilt is 7 blocks long, it will measure 42½", which is about the width of fabric from selvage to selvage. Measure, cut, and sew the inner and outer borders to the side of the quilt. Press toward the outside edge.

If your quilt is 6 blocks wide, it will measure 36½". Cut borders using this measurement. In addition, cut 4 squares 3½" x 3½" from the outer border fabric for each corner. Attach a 3½" strip of narrow border to 1 side of each of the 4 squares. Next, sew a 4¾" piece to the other side of the 4 squares (this assumes an inner border that is cut 1¾" wide and finishes at 1¼" wide). Keep in mind that 2 of the corner squares will go on the top and 2 on the bottom, as shown.

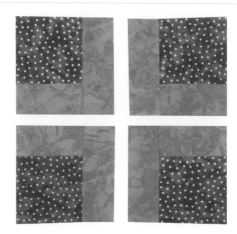

Pieces for the border corners

If your quilt is larger, you will need to piece the border. If you are using a print fabric, try to piece so it isn't obvious that you did so.

Batting

Cotton batting is thin, flat, and easy to machine quilt. If you are making a wallhanging, it is easier to make the quilt lie flat if you use all-cotton batting. You may also use a thin cotton/polyester batting. Wool batting is excellent, but quite a bit more expensive.

When you cut batting, always allow about 3" extra on all four sides of your quilt. This makes it much easier to work with when basting.

Backing

For the backing, try to use a printed fabric that contains colors that blend with the quilt. If you use a solid-color piece, all your machine quilting will show up on the back. If you are a beginner at machine quilting, a print will disguise less-than-perfect stitches.

If your quilt measures more than 40" wide, you will need to piece your backing. You may need to use two fabrics if you are working out of your stash. If you need to piece, do not just sew a piece on the edge or insert it in the middle. That makes it look like you didn't have enough fabric. Arrange your fabrics in a pleasing manner and sew them together or piece them off-center and call it "back art."

Lay your quilt backing wrong side up, place the batting on top, and smooth out any wrinkles. Add your pressed quilt top and baste with thread for hand quilting or use rust-proof safety pins for machine quilting.

Quilting

If you are a beginner, it's a good idea to buy a book on quilting or to take a beginner quilting class at a local quilt shop. All the quilts in this book are machine quilted because it is a much faster way to complete the quilt. Of course, you may hand quilt if that is your preference.

Free-motion quilting looks great on these quilts! Try following the larger designs, or simply make large leaves, flowers, stars, or stipple quilt. Quilt the body of the quilt first, then the borders. Stitch in-the-ditch (along seamlines) between the quilt and the border and between the inner and outer borders. Always quilt in the outer border, even if it's just a couple of straight lines. If the quilt is quilted and the border is not, it will not lie flat! Even if you have measured perfectly, you will need some quilting in the border.

Binding

These instructions are for double-fold, straight-grain binding (also called French Fold binding). It will finish a scant ½" wide.

1. Trim excess batting and backing from the quilt.

2. Cut binding strips 2½" wide; you will need enough to go around the sides of your quilt plus 12". Piece together with a diagonal seam to make a continuous binding strip. Press the seams open, then press the entire strip in half lengthwise with wrong sides together.

3. With raw edges even, pin the binding to the edge of the quilt a few inches away from the corner, and leave the first few inches of the binding unattached. Start sewing, using a ¼" seam allowance.

4. Stop ¼" away from the first corner, as shown; backstitch one stitch. Lift the presser foot and needle. Rotate the quilt one quarter turn. Fold the binding at a right angle so it extends straight above the quilt. Then bring the binding strip down even with the edge of the quilt. Begin sewing at the folded edge. Repeat in the same manner at all corners.

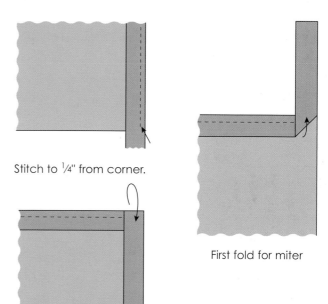

Stitch to ¼" from corner.

First fold for miter

Second fold alignment

5. When you reach the last side, fold under the beginning end of the binding strip ¼". Lay the ending binding strip over the beginning folded end. Continue stitching beyond the folded edge. Trim the excess binding. Fold the binding over the raw edges to the quilt back and hand stitch, mitering the corners.

About the Author

Photo by Susie Ernst

Judy Sisneros's first memory of sewing is of making doll clothes as a child. Her first sewing lessons began with the birth of her first daughter in 1964. She began quilting in 1987, taking quilt classes at a local adult school (the first class was called "Manipulative Skills for the Mature Adult").

After a move to California's far north coast, she began making landscape quilts. Her first book, *Simply Landscapes*, was published in 1994. Judy has been teaching since 1993 and feels fortunate to be making a living doing something she loves.

Judy's workshops include landscape quilts, quilts using traditional blocks in a nontraditional way, and original design blocks. She is available to teach and lecture nationwide. Her love of people, travel, and fabric makes her an enthusiastic teacher! Kits are available for purchase. Check her website at www.judysisneros.com.

Judy has three grown children and seven grandchildren. She lives in Rocklin, California, near Sacramento.